J'MEL L. JOHNSON

QUOTES & J😂KES

A MENTAL DETOX FOR TWEENS & TEENS

Quotes & Jokes:

A Mental Detox for Tweens & Teens

Author: J'Mel L. Johnson

Dedication:

This book is dedicated to all of my past, present and future students.
Thank you for inspiring me. Above anything else, I wish that you will be mentally,
emotionally, & physically well, and reach your
fullest potential in life.

First edition October 2021

ISBN 979-8-218-08177-5 (paperback)

Special Note

Dear Special Person,

Guess what? YOU are very special. What's most important though, is that YOU know it. Even though I just told you that *you are very special*, it doesn't matter if *you* still don't believe it. Whatever you think you are, it's true. Notice I said, whatever "you" think...not what I think, your parents, your friends, or family members think. It all comes down to YOUR thinking.

THINK... To think means to direct your mind towards something or someone. Well, I want you to direct your mind towards you; your thoughts, your words, and your views. Your life will reflect your words and thoughts. So, now is the time to truly reflect on what you have been thinking and what you have been telling yourself. As you begin this journey, think about your life experiences. Reflect on the good and not-so-good choices you've made, and just take some time evaluating the outcomes. Were they fair or expected? Did you get the results you intended to get? What did you learn from the experience? What would you do differently if you were faced with the same situation again?

Your thinking will continue to evolve as you mature and have more life experiences. I am hopeful that this collection of quotes and short stories I've written will be a part of your journey, and be a benefit to your life for many years to come. You will begin to think differently about your words, thoughts, and actions. You will be more aware of how you treat people, as well as how you allow other people to treat you. Your thinking will change for the better as this mental detox filters out all of the stuff that has been holding you back from being the best version of you.

The jokes are inserted just for giggles and laughs. Laughter is like Vitamin D for the soul. It's one of those rare things in life that is a great benefit at no cost. Sure some of the jokes are a bit cheesy, but, you may get a few good laughs. Better yet, use them to cheer up little kids, or the elderly. Making others smile and laugh also benefits you. By the way, if you are a *doodler*, take advantage of the **free space** pages at the end of the book. That's yet another way to detox and free up some mental space. So, let the journey begin!

DAY 1:

"Your attitude is a choice."

My mother used to say to my siblings and me all the time, "Fix your attitude!" or "What's wrong with you?" I would always respond by blaming one of my sisters or someone else. In my mind, it was always someone else's fault if I was in a bad mood. At the time, I never considered that the person I blamed was not the *reason* for my attitude. It was because I gave up my power to choose, and I left it at the mercy of the offender. It's actually very funny now when I think back on it. Why would I give away something I had the power to control?

Maybe you can relate to my experience, and you too have given this power away. If so, take it back! Decide today that you will never again give it away. Make the decision that you will choose the attitude **YOU** want to have, regardless of what someone else says or does, or what challenge you face. Don't allow anyone or any circumstance to ruin your moment, your day or your experience.

Task: Take some time to reflect and journal your thoughts. How you will intentionally choose your attitude? (Example: walk away, ignore, etc.)

_____

_____

_____

_____

_____

_____

_____

_____

_____

Day 1 Joke: Why did the banana go to the doctor?

DAY 2:

"Each choice you make determines the outcome of your days, weeks, years, and ultimately your destiny."

Choices, choices, choices. Even in a world where it seems like our choices are slowly being taken away from us, guess what? We still make tons of choices every single day. For example, you choose your attitude, you choose to get up on time or hit the snooze, you choose to exercise or sit around, you choose how you will reply to a message, you choose how much effort you will put into your work, and the list goes on. It has been estimated that the average young adult makes around 35,000 minimally-conscious decisions each day.[1] If you are making that many daily choices, there's no doubt your life is influenced by them. Think about how your daily choices have affected your day or week so far.

TASK: Below, journal your thoughts as to whether you think your choices have had positive or negative outcomes. Are you getting the results you want? If you're not getting the results you desire, be more intentional about your daily decisions. What changes can you make?

_____

_____

_____

_____

_____

_____

_____

_____

_____

Answer to Day 1: Because it wasn't peeling well.
   Day 2 Joke: What is a snowman's favorite cereal?

DAY 3:

"The way you feel today is a result of what you meditated on yesterday."

Meditation is good for the mind. However, if you meditate on the wrong things, you can do damage. When you meditate, you make an effort to concentrate and focus your thoughts on something. The good news is you can CHOOSE what you give your thoughts to. My *personal* definition of meditating is fueling your brain with energy that can be put to good use so that you have the desired mood and feelings you want to have. If you meditate on the wrong things, you will surely end up in a bad headspace, which will ultimately determine your mood and the energy you give off. So, before you began to meditate on any thought, remember this rule of meditation: good thoughts in, good feelings out, and bad thoughts in, bad feelings out. Now, it's time to practice.

<u>TODAY'S TASK</u>: **Meditate on and repeat the phrase below over and over:**
Today I choose to be happy.

Now complete the phrases below to enhance your mood:
1. I feel happiest when I am:
2. The people I am happiest around are:
3. My happy place is:
4. The last time I laughed really hard was when:

Answer to Day 2: frosted flakes

Day 3 Joke: What do you call the sibling of a peanut?

DAY 4:

"The more excuses you make, the more average you become."

Think of all of the excuses you have made in the past. Now think about what they all add up to. I bet you get nothing. Excuses add up to absolutely NOTHING. No one gains anything from excuses. They are just empty, useless words. So since excuses don't add up to anything, then that means they subtract and take away. They take away from your time, your will, your efforts, your dreams, your goals, and your purpose. Excuses take away from **EVERYTHING**. Excuses make you blend in with the world. You will never stand out at anything if you never push yourself beyond your excuses. "I would have, **but,**"... "I should have, **but,**"..."I was going to, **but,**"...but...but...but... **BUTS stink!** (No pun intended). No more buts! Make up your mind today that you will NOT make any more excuses.

<u>TASK</u>: **Below, create an image of you kicking your "buts" out of the way.**

_____
_____
_____
_____
_____
_____
_____
_____
_____
_____
_____

Answer to Day 3: *a peanut brutter*

Day 4 Joke: *What do you call a fake noodle?*

DAY 5:

"Your beliefs lead to your behavior."

Your beliefs began to develop at a very young age. For example, when my mother was a little girl, she had a bad experience with a dog, and she had a negative view of all dogs after that. Fast-forward, years later, my mom passed down her fear of dogs to my siblings and me. My mom would say, "Stay away from dogs because they're dangerous, and they bite." Even though I had never had a bad experience personally with a dog, I would tense up and become very afraid every time I saw one. Ultimately, my mother's views led to my behavior. It took years, but eventually the fear of dogs dissolved once I had several positive interactions and experiences. My mother's views were no longer mine. Maybe your experience wasn't with a dog, but maybe you have had biases towards people because of race, culture or a lifestyle different from your own; maybe these views have led you to treat them with hatred, or behave negatively towards them.

TASK: **Write about how some of your beliefs have led to your behavior.** If there are any behaviors you want to change, brainstorm and write down some ways you will begin to make some changes.

_____

_____

_____

_____

_____

_____

_____

_____

Answer to Day 4: *an impasta*

Day 5 Joke: *Where do cows go for entertainment?*

DAY 6:

"The world is filled with individual classrooms."

Every classroom is filled with different life stories. In class, you may come across people whose culture, values, or beliefs are different from your own. This is how individual classrooms or opportunities to learn are created. Different doesn't mean bad. Differences are great when they are embraced. For instance, when you have a difference of opinion or belief as another person, it challenges you to see things from their perspective, and this also challenges the other person to see things from yours. Ultimately, even if you don't agree, be open to learn. Reflect on a time you and someone else had differences of opinion. Did you learn something new? Did you change your point of view? Did you influence someone else to change their view?

TASK: Use the chart below to reflect on one of your experiences.

My initial point of view: How it changed:

At first....	Now I.....
_____	_____
_____	_____
_____	_____
_____	_____
_____	_____
_____	_____

Answer to Day 5: To the moo-vies

Day 6 Joke: What travels all around the world but stays in one place?

DAY 7:

"Unfair rules are a result of compliant people."

Have you ever gone along with a rule even though you didn't think it was fair? For example, maybe an unreasonable dress code is enforced at school, or maybe you don't get a break in between classes. A compliant person will at times cooperate unwillingly because the opposition is in power or authority. In other words, compliance is the act of obeying out of feeling powerless, and not necessarily because of agreement. So if you do not agree, find others who share your view. Alone, you may feel defeated, but together change is possible, because there is strength in numbers.

If you feel that you've been following an unfair (biased) rule or procedure, then you should start a petition. If you don't know how to start a petition, see the sample below. As you can see, you will need to have supporters sign your petition. After you collect your 5, 10, 30 or 100 signatures, respectfully submit it to the authorizing source, and advocate for change. Whatever the issue is, don't sit back, complain or be compliant. Instead, be the one to initiate the change.

*SAMPLE PETITION: write or type your own and get as many signatures as you can

Petition for change: We the undersigned are concerned citizens who urge you to consider changing the school dress code because we believe it is gender bias.

Name:	Signature:	Date:
1. Jane Doe	*Jane Doe*	1/1/2022
2. Tom Doe	*Tom Doe*	1/1/2022

Answer to Day 6: a stamp

Day 7 Joke: What did the football coach say to the broken vending machine?

DAY 8:

"If you're always ahead, you'll never get behind."

Time is fair. Everyone gets the same 24 hours each day. Time doesn't stop for anyone; it just keeps moving. You can't control time, but you can control how you use it. For instance, arriving to practice early to get some extra one-to-one practice with your coach helps you get better at the game. Spending extra time practicing your craft or skill will help you improve your level of ability.

Some people are always getting behind because they wait until the last minute. However, turning in projects early, will reduce the stress and worry of being late. Plus if you get work done ahead of time, you'll have more time to hang out with friends, or to do something fun. Whatever the situation is, you can get ahead by planning how you will use your time. Time is moving along right now. Will you use it wisely and get ahead today?

TASK: Come up with ways to use your time more wisely.
 Example: I will start my science project the day I get it so that I can finish it before the due date.

#1:

#2:

#3:

#4:

Answer to Day 7: *Give me my quarterback!*

 Day 8 Joke: *How come ants never get sick?*

DAY 9:

"The word UNIQUE doesn't exist without U."

You put the "U" in Unique. Each individual person is creatively different on purpose. Did you know that no one else has your DNA, fingerprint, taste buds, or eyeballs? The shape of your ears, the tone of voice, your personality, your creativity, your emotions, and so much more, are all traits that make you special. Learn to love and accept yourself and all of your uniqueness. When you are not concerned or worried about other people's opinions of you, then that makes you even more special because it shows that you have embraced who you are. Instead of trying to fit in, celebrate your uniqueness. Each earthly being is a special gift to the world. So from this day on, know that you are a gift! What are some things about yourself that you are most proud of?

I am most proud of:

-
-
-
-

Answer to Day 8: *Because they have little antibodies.*

Day 9 Joke: *Why do bees have sticky hair?*

DAY 10:

"The more confident you are, the less you focus on the competition."

How can you ever truly recognize the unique and awesome person that you are if you're always trying to measure yourself up to the competition? Even as much as Kobe Bryant admired Michael Jordan, Kobe was not intimidated by Jordan. Jordan even said, "Kobe gave every last ounce of himself to whatever he was doing." Kobe was more focused on becoming a better version of himself. You can apply this same lesson to your life. Be your own competition. Always strive to be the best version of YOU that you can be.

Say these positive affirmations to motivate yourself:
I am special.
I am unique.
My life is valuable and important.
No one else is like me.
I get better, stronger, and smarter every day.

_____

Answer to Day 9: *Because they use a honeycomb.*

Day 10 Joke: *Why was the math book sad?*

DAY 11:

"There are no restrictions on your imagination."

I know you've been told you can't do certain things. Maybe even for your safety, your parent or caregiver has restricted you from going on certain websites, or has set limits on what you can do and where you can go. Even though restrictions are everywhere, there is one thing that no one can put limits on, and that is your imagination. Imagination is the freedom to think and create. Maybe your imagination is waiting to create the next big idea of the future. When you have some quiet time, close your eyes and just let your imagination go. When you are done, write down everything you imagined. Nothing is too big to imagine, so think BIG and bold without any restrictions on your creative thinking.

> In my mind,
> I can see ...

_____

_____

_____

_____

_____

_____

_____

_____

_____

_____

_____

Answer to Day 10: *Because it had too many problems.*

Day 11 Joke: *What kind of books will you find in outer space?*

DAY 12:

"We all have emotions.
Just don't let your emotions have you."

We all respond in our own way to life's issues, situations and challenges. Learning how to control our emotional responses to our problems is where things get tricky. First, let me say that your emotions are real and they should be validated. However, just keep in mind that when there is a problem, your emotions are the reaction, not the solution. If you stay caught up in your emotions, your problems won't get solved. Once you have gotten all of your emotions out, pull yourself together, get a hold of yourself, and work on coming up with a plan or solution. Don't allow your emotions to have the best of you. Remember, you are still responsible for your reaction, your behavior, and for the choices you make.

Acknowledge how you are feeling today.
Today I feel: (circle one)

Happy	Sad	Frustrated	Excited	Other:
☺	☹	😐	😆	

Think: How will I get a hold of my emotions today? (Circle one)

Talk to someone who can help   Self-talk   Take deep breaths   Count down

Share my good news   Spread these good vibes   Other: (_____)

Answer to Day 11: Comet books

Day 12 Joke: *Why was 6 afraid of 7?*

DAY 13:

"Your thoughts are the compass of your life."

Every thought creates a pathway. Never devalue your thoughts; they are a very valuable commodity. You can never think too big, because ANYTHING is possible! Everything that exists started in someone's mind, thoughts and imagination (phones, airplanes, computers, chairs, etc.). The world is waiting for YOUR influence. Where will your thoughts take you? What book, song, movie script, or artwork will you create? What cure or invention will you come up with? Spend some time today **thinking** and **creating** the life you want to have. Write down your thoughts, visions and plans.

Thoughts and reflections:

_____

_____

_____

_____

_____

_____

_____

_____

_____

_____

_____

_____

Answer to Day 12: Because 7, 8 (ate), 9

Day 13 Joke: What kind of pets does a band have?

DAY 14:

"If you're listening you're not talking, and if you're talking, you're not listening."

It's impossible to listen and speak at the same time. Sure you can still *hear* and talk at the same time, but definitely not listen. Listening means you are fully focused, concentrated, and attentive to what is being said. Listening is the most critical part of communication. So, to be the most effective at listening, stop talking. The world is full of talkers. I once heard someone say that the reason we have one mouth and two ears is so that we can listen more than we speak. There is so much value in listening. You may rarely be celebrated for being a good listener, but you will certainly be appreciated!

- Are you a better listener or talker?
- Do you have trouble waiting your turn to talk?
- Do you cut people off in conversations?

Activity to practice:
The next time you are having a conversation with someone, make a mental note of how many times you interrupt, or may have wanted to interrupt the person speaking. Do this every time you are engaged in a conversation, because the more you recognize it, the better you will become at controlling the urge to interrupt, and you will ultimately become a better listener.

Answer to Day 13: Trumpets

Day 14 Joke: *Why did the egg go to school?*

DAY 15:

"Your energy speaks before you ever say a word."

Maybe you've heard the phrase, "First impressions are lasting impressions." Well, I have found this to be true. People will always remember what they thought of you the first time they met you. They will usually start off the conversation with statements like, "The day we met, you were so nice."… or… "You were so calm & cool when we first met."…or… "I thought you were mean when I first met you."

Notice that nothing truly had anything to do with what you said or didn't say. It's the energy! People will judge you by the vibes they get being around you. So keep in mind that your energy is a powerful method of communication, and it speaks louder than words. Your vibe is also one of the most memorable things about your personality.

<u>TASK</u>: **Reflect on some 1st impressions you had of people** (a teacher, a coach, a teammate, a classmate). **These should be a combination of good and bad impressions that were made. Write the person's name and what you first thought of the person.**

-
-
-
-

Answer to Day 14: To get an *eggucation.*

Day 15 Joke: Where do spiders like to hang out?

DAY 16:

"Put pressure on your purpose."

At this point in your life, you may have already discovered that one thing you get the most joy or pleasure out of doing - maybe it's skateboarding, dancing, or playing a sport like basketball or soccer. Maybe it's drawing, painting, or creating funny videos. Whatever it is, if you wake up thinking about it and you go to bed dreaming about it, then that just may be your passion or purpose in life. Putting pressure on your purpose simply means to intentionally work on that *thing* with the most effort. The fact that you exist on this earth is proof that you have a purpose for being here. So put the pressure on your purpose until you are at your personal BEST! Spend at least thirty minutes each day working on a skill or talent that you have. Find a mentor, read books, or find information on the internet. Whatever you do, go after it intensely, and don't stop until you succeed!

I am really good at_____,
and if I intentionally put effort and work into it, I can be very successful.

I will work to become my personal best at_____.
I am going to do this by _____
_____

Answer to Day 15: *On websites*

Day 16 Joke: *Why do we tell actors to break a leg?*

DAY 17:

"Be the person that people are happy to see coming and sad to see leaving."

Some people have a way of making others laugh and feel happy every time they are around. Maybe for you, it's that favorite family member, friend, or teacher. This is the person that just has a way of turning your frown upside down. Unfortunately, others have a way of destroying the fun, and ruining a good time. These are generally people who bully, complain, criticize, tease or just simply like to start drama. Which person are you? Do you bring joy, pain, sunshine or rain? Next time you walk into a room, assess the energy. Are people happy to see you coming, or do you find that most people stay far away from you? Are you the person who smiles, greets others and give compliments, or are you the person insulting others, making mean jokes, and complaining about everything? It's time to be real with yourself so that you can make the necessary adjustments. It's never too late. Humans are known to be the most adaptable creatures on earth.

MOOD METER

1. The last time I walked into a room people felt....

Frustrated	Uncomfortable	Relaxed	Happy	Excited

2. I know this because...

3. If it was a good reaction, that's great! Keep it up. If it was a not a good reaction, what will you do to make the mood more positive next time?

Answer to Day 16: *Because every show has a cast.*

Day 17 Joke: *How does the ocean say Good Morning?*

DAY 18:

"Everybody is somebody."

All humans are made up of the same six elements that make up the galaxy (oxygen, carbon, hydrogen, nitrogen, calcium, and phosphorus). So in actuality, we are all made of "STARDUST". In other words, there is **STAR POWER** in each and every individual. Right now at this very moment, you may be sitting next to a future president, astronaut, scientist, songwriter, superstar, or maybe your BOSS. STAR POWER is in each and "every" human-being. Looking down on people because of how they dress, how they look, or for what they have and don't have, is a HUGE mistake! Always keep in mind that there is a STAR in everyone, including YOU. We all SHINE in our own special way!

TASK: Draw a galaxy of stars. Make a star that represents YOU in the galaxy. Make your star shine in its own special way.

Answer to Day 17: It waves

Day 18 Joke: Why did the baseball player get arrested?

DAY 19:

"Just because it's reasonable doesn't mean it's right."

The truth is we can give ourselves a reason to do anything. We can convince ourselves that our reason is justified or valid. For example, someone calls you a very disrespectful or inappropriate name, so you physically assault the person. Your *reason* for hurting the person physically was because you were offended and emotionally hurt by the person's words. However, does this mean that physical retaliation was the *right* thing to do? Sometimes the things we do that seem reasonable, can lead to short and long-term, negative consequences. So, before you go through with your actions, stop and ask yourself these questions: Is this the **right** thing to do? Could my reasoning possibly result in negative consequences? If you answered yes and yes, then it is probably not the *best choice for you to make.* Always think about how your choices will affect you and whether or not your decisions will result in the consequences you want.

TASK: Read the questions below, and then circle your answer.
1. Which side are you usually pulled to?   Reasonable or Right
2. Most times I am happy with the decisions I make.   Yes or No

If you circled _Reasonable_ for #1 and _No_ for #2, then take some time to go review the strategies you read on Day 12 to help guide your decision making.

Answer to Day 18: For stealing a base

Day 19 Joke: *How do you get a squirrel to like you?*

DAY 20:

"Every day you wake up is a good day."

Smile! ☺ Why? You woke up today, that's why. Of course, there are situations that can come up throughout the day, situations that can challenge or make your day difficult. However, it doesn't mean it's a bad day. The fact that you woke up still makes it a good day! Whenever I find myself feeling down or upset, I think about all the people that didn't wake up, the people who thought they had more time, and the people who never got to accomplish their dreams. When I wake up, it reminds me that I still have more time, more opportunities, and more chances to try again. Remember that *life* is a precious gift. Be grateful and take advantage of it every day. One way to be appreciative of life is to make a grateful list. Make a list each day which includes all of the things you are thankful for (like oxygen, eyesight, flowers, family, etc.). Reminders of the joys & blessings of life will bring some positive energy to your day.

Grateful List:

-
-
-
-
-
-
-

Answer to Day 19: *Act like a nut.*

Day 20 Joke: *What do you call a train carrying bubble gum?*

DAY 21:

"Weapons were not designed to resolve internal battles."

The military uses weapons to serve and protect against enemy attacks and to fight when in battle. In those situations, weapons are being used for their intended purpose (to serve and protect).   Weapons on the other hand, were not designed to fight emotional battles. **Using violence and *weapons to harm others or to do self-harm will <u>never</u> resolve your issues*.**   In fact, it could lead to severe consequences.

If you ever deal with a situation that brings on so much distress that you start thinking about hurting yourself or others, there are ways to get help. Start with talking to a trusted adult you are familiar and comfortable with; like a parent, guardian, coach, mentor, school counselor, a nurse, a doctor, or a teacher. I'm sure that one of these trusted adults will guide and help you. Also, on day 12, you were given ways to handle emotions. Those strategies will help decrease the intensity of negative emotions before they lead to uncontrollable behavior or violence.

<u>TASK:</u> Fill out the plan of action written below so that you will have it if you ever need it. It's always best to be prepared.

Plan of Action:

If I find myself getting emotionally out of control, I will talk to:

_____ or _____.

(Person's name)   (Person's name)

Answer to Day 20: A chew-chew train.

Day 21 Joke: Why did the teacher jump in the pool?

DAY 22:

"Hard? Yes. Difficult? Absolutely. Impossible? Not a chance!"

You have finally reached the last day, and I truly hope that you have learned some lessons that will stick with you throughout your life. You will have days when you will not fully follow through with doing what you know is right to do, and that is okay because NO ONE is perfect. There is always tomorrow to try again. Will there be difficult days that will make you feel like quitting? ABSOLUTELY! But, when those moments come, do not allow your emotions to get the best of you.   Remember that you are unique, and that you are somebody. Your very existence on this earth MATTERS! Failing is inevitable, but quitting is optional. Winning at your goals may be challenging, but not impossible! So don't ever quit, lose hope or give up.

Self-Reflection:

What lessons can I learn from losing or failing?

How can I improve?

What do I need to change or do differently?

Now, repeat these positive affirmations:

I am a learner, not a loser.

I am a winner. I was born to win. Winning is in my DNA.

I am smart. I make good decisions.

I am stronger today than I was yesterday.

Nothing is impossible.

Answer to Day 21: To test the waters

Day 22 Joke: How do birds communicate with technology?

Final note

Dear Special Person,

CONGRATULATIONS! You made it to the end of this mental detox. Stardust is probably shining on your face, and your mind is feeling refreshed and renewed. Chances are your mental space is now filled with positivity, creativity, and you are feeling motivated to be an even better version of yourself. So, I have a few questions for you to think about. Which quote did you connect to the most? How has your mindset changed? What actions have you taken over the past 22 days to promote positivity in your life? What actions do you plan to take in the future?

Don't stop here! Today, make a plan to keep this positive mindset. Here are a few suggestions: Reread this mental detox, recite the quotes over and over again, create a positive affirmation journal and recite the positive phrases daily, and/or find other resources that promote renewing your mind. Most importantly, protect your peace. Don't allow any negativity into your headspace.

Lastly, spread the positive energy. Tell someone else about this book. Tell a friend, a classmate or anyone you know could use it. Maybe even share it with a teacher or your school's guidance counselor. The same way it has impacted your life, it will hopefully impact someone else's life in the same way. So help someone else find the path to living and thinking more positively. Whenever you share this book, please use the following hashtags to show your support. #quotesandjokes #mentaldetox

Remember, you're Amazing!

Answer to Day 22: They send tweets.

MEET THE AUTHOR

J'Mel Johnson is a wife, mother, teacher, singer, songwriter, author and a mentor. She has a love for life, people, good music, and great energy. She has a special passion for motivating older children and teens; inspiring them, and teaching them how to protect their positive energy and space. She has been a classroom teacher and educator for 20+ years, and this experience has shown her how to connect with "tweens and teens" and how to relate to their perspective. Raising children of her own has given her the parental lens, which helps her deliver these life-lessons in a nurturing way.

Acknowledgements

It took me two years to get the courage up to finish this book. I needed to find the courage to believe that I had something valuable to share outside of the 4 walls of my classroom. I eventually convinced myself that my students weren't the only ones I needed to serve with much needed encouragement & inspiration. I am very grateful for the help I received from willing and caring individuals around me. Without the help, encouragement, guidance and motivation from these superstar individuals, this now published book, would still be locked away in my journal.

First, I want to thank my husband, Tommy, for believing in me even when I doubted myself. I also want to thank you for reading all 19 versions of this book (Haha!). You are truly my soul-mate and inspiration, I love you immensely. Next I want to thank my mentor, Catresa Myers. And I am forever grateful to you for your encouragement, guidance and sacrifice of your time. You are truly a gem, as well as a phenomenal writer! I also want to thank my boys, Mir and Myles. You guys were Mom's first teen critics and cheering squad. You both know how much I love you. Thanks for being there for me! Thank you Maddy, David, Jordan & Ethan for giving up your time to help make this book become teen approved! Thank you to my Mom, Dad and all of my family & friends (you know who you are) for your love, encouragement & support. I love you all deeply. Thank you to my friends and colleagues, who took time to share your feedback, edits, and encouragement (Brian, Lucretia, Trina, Debbie, Jen, Erik, Mindy, Dawn, Marty, Dr. Jenna Rufo, Dr. Barbara Moore-Williams, & the writer's club members). I am forever grateful for your invaluable help. Also, thank you so much Monica Stanley, Gift of Graphics LLC, for seeing the vision and creating this lively cover. You are truly a gift!

Lastly, thank you to all of my students (past and present). You have all helped me to be a better listener, mentor, educator and influencer. I love you all. During these 20+ years, I've learned how to see the best and bring out the BEST in everyone I work with. I have also learned to say that you are ALL my "favorites" ☺.

Bibliography

[1] https://www.Science.unctv.org

[2] Si.com (Sports Illustrated) https://www.si.com/nba/lakers/news/michael-jordan-says-kobe-bryant-couldve-beaten-him-one-on-one

A Letter to Parents, Caretakers, and Educators:
Dear Caring Individual,

A few years ago I had my own personal mind shift as a parent and as an educator. I stopped asking my children and my students the infamous question, "What do you want to be when you grow up?" I realized that a more important question needed to be asked. It was the year I had a student who told me that she wanted to open her own bakery one day. I was a bit concerned because she struggled with controlling her anger and temper. She often lashed out at her peers (screaming and yelling whenever she got angry). I realized that she had goals, dreams and aspirations.

I couldn't help but to think that if she didn't get control of her emotions, she may not be as successful as she intended to be. So this prompted me to ask her this next question. I said, "So what *kind* of person will you be when you grow up?" She looked at me a bit puzzled. I said, "Well, will you be kind, patient, and compassionate?" She looked like she was beginning to understand me. I ended this conversation by saying, "What will it benefit you to become a business owner and you treat your customers the way you've been treating your classmates?" I asked, "Do you think those customers will come back?" The puzzled look was replaced by a look of concern. I knew then that I had her full attention. The next day, she told me that she had decided she was going to work harder on changing her attitude.

That is what inspired me to create this book. I want all of the young people we are raising, teaching, and mentoring to see that there is just as much (and maybe even more) value in character and integrity as there is in intellect and talent. Just like my 6th grade student decided that she wanted to change, I believe this is a decision all of our youth can make once they have been inspired and challenged to shift their thinking. As both an educator for 20+ years, and presently a parent of teenagers, I have witnessed the many times our youth have played *the blame game*. What most adolescents have learned up to this point is that blame is always successful. By blaming others, they successfully take the pressure and the heat off of themselves for that moment. However, what is yet to be learned is that blame is never helpful. Some of the best lessons in life come from taking responsibility for your words and choices.

Responsibility and *accountability* are trigger words for most adolescents. They don't like to hear their name in a sentence with either of these words. However, through this collection of the most thought-provoking quotes that I've written, my hope is that their minds will go through a detox, and that they will become adolescents who assume accountability for their words, thoughts and actions from here on out. No boring lecture, speech, or lesson, but short inspirational quotes, and several mind-shifting activities, that will help your tween and/or teen do some self-evaluating, which will lead to a mental cleansing... a mind shift, and having a teen who will stop, think, and reflect, on their behaviors and actions without any prompting. Oh the joy!

I'm sure you've heard the saying, "laughter is medicine for the soul." I have had some serious, intense conversations with my students; like the ones after the cafeteria assistant tells you that your class was throwing food or being obnoxiously loud (yes, those conversations). Well after one of those serious, reprimanding conversations, I would always end with a funny comment or joke, and then, *VOILA*! ....just like a sprinkle of fairy dust, they are back in good spirits, smiling, laughing, and ready to learn. So the jokes are embedded to keep the energy positive. Some of the quotes may lead to serious, deep moments of self-reflection. A little burst of laughter will reboot and reset their mood. I hope you now have the understanding that this isn't a book filled with a bunch of positive phrases and sayings.

These quotes were formed with the intent of helping our future leaders develop and mature into self-aware, responsible, and thoughtful adults. This little book of inspiration will provoke each reader to think about their future self, and to be more focused on developing character, rather than skill and talent. I like to think of this as a mental flush that rids the mind of those bad thoughts, ideas, and perceptions. Finally, these motivational memos will help teens move towards progress-not perfection. Change and growth will be inevitable. So I hope that you can recognize a change in your teen after they have finished this book. This could also be for your niece, nephew, neighbor, or hey, maybe it's for you! We can all benefit from *a mental detox*.

FREE SPACE

FREE SPACE

_____

_____

_____

_____

_____

_____

_____

_____

_____

_____

_____

_____

_____

_____

_____

_____

_____

_____

_____

_____

_____

_____

FREE SPACE